Certain Lightnings

By Scott Krieger

Cover Design by Tim Calkins
https://timcalkinscreative.com

ISBN 978-1-968226-05-3

Grand River Poetry Press
Grand Rapids, Michigan, USA
grandriverpoetrycollective.com

For the friends and family
who called them forth,
and always, Christine

Contents

Thresholds

Reckonings

Openings

Thresholds

Power Line Prophets

This blinding yellow tail—
singing some measure only he knows
at the treetop's edge,
washed of sorrow in the gold light—

His year's work finished.
Fledglings flicker,
almost gone in the spilled
sunset swallowing them.

Invader starling—
wings thrash, clatter tin cans,
scrape the scene.

They fall on the last of the serviceberries—
All hunger, all flight.
A racket of song spurs them away,
sure of sky—

Where will they go
when winter howls on the wires?
Stuttering prophecies
with windy certainty.

Sanctity sacrificed
in February—
relearned, shameless
in the wrecked blooms of May.

First Time

I am too soon
a startled bass—

a boat,
an oar,
a pale moon hung low on the shore—

a broken pledge
rushed down the gutter
into the gullet of a crow.

Let the tide
drown my song.
I don't want your lips—but you.

Over the hooded nose, through
the tangle
of a fallen lock—

to find
in a moment of panic,
a moment of delight.

But the dawn—
that universe
closes in—

But the rain—
my lips gape, then purse.
Let the water down, my only hope.

We,
and our hollowed-out excuses
relent into a quivering huddle.

Still,
never free of our fear—
you opened your body to me

and we shook—
river-slick,
quick-flashing in the bilge,
for a new glory.

Dream Launch

The night,
too hard for love,
she pulls away.
Alone again, he rises.

Here's a corner crust of morning toast,
regret spread like butter,
a nagging taste
that doesn't speak.

Here,
a thin film of milk
in a mason jar.

A jaundiced sun
caught dreaming—
a peach pit,
a knotted curl.

The horizon—
a knitting needle
the length of Ethiopia.

Frayed threads off her gown—
unfurl late—
to deep, enticing tears.

The dream—oh God,
the holy, heaving wish—
a seam rifted open in the sky,

The rain tramples flowers.
Others rise.
Lightning jerks
across the night.

The thread remains,
a shadow folded up
and stuck
like a wet leaf.

Something dances,
inflated by desire,
he can't
let loose—

What could be
a red balloon
cruising over May blossoms,

brickwork,
broken plateaus,
plots of tulips—

over cars crossing side streets,

Dairy Queens,
children questioning
over cones—

the dream of altitude
released beyond cloudy faces—

The Signal, Passing Through

New genesis star chart—
steer my hand
clear from the dirt-eat-dirt of the last world,
sipapu, old wound—

guide me
out of the underworld,
through half-built
megalith memories.

Mud-blooded
with new medicine,
machine-clutched,
passing through a hole in the ceiling,

passing through
keyholes of deeper darkness,
chasing idea into being.
What once was the future retreating.

Wind throws powder snow.
We stand by, cast in a crystal vortex,
just beyond the shell of our senses,
in the wee small hours,

searching the sky's belly
for late-night station WLS
ghosting over the lake from Chicago.
Distressed wavelengths squelch away

resolve into testimony—
Amplitudes beamed off the sky
to deliver their medicine
only for the lonely.

An eternal void sea glitters,
flush against a black sky.
Channels of intention
scatter and glance unseen

until a crystal harness grabs the signal—
locks in a note
so mellow and fine
it could speak for all of us.

Kairos Wind

For my father

Child of promise,
pushed ahead
just in time
to slip out,

go—
lay down your noose,
make fresh promise
to the widening blue,

mercenary storm-cloud,
thunder for hire,
take the marching cure
over bastinado badlands.

The wind and wave break quick
to drive new doubts away—
You'll fend them off
when the hour arrives.

A steel beginner must
learn from the raw wind,
keep an open transom
to the star field.

Greet the dawn glow,
taste the salt off Gibraltar
where a glimmer of silk
cuts the light,
spells the sea.

Djinn at the Bar

for Stephen Durst

You'll find me nowhere
but in this bottle.
This could all be a dream—
a handmade fantasy.

Wasn't that me?
Gawking from the hillside
beyond the barking dogs—
staring down a solitary tree.

I drifted off on an ice floe.
In the dark
of night's open nothing,
I heard the solemn trickle
of a thousand streams
condense
into the timeless sea.

You could ask for
your three wishes—
but there are so many things
I can't do for you.

Here,
in the face of the infinite,
we are drawn
into the particulars.

What you can gather,
despite the emptiness—
that wholeness,
though just a bitter drop,
is yours.

Logs Full of Ghosts

1.

Web site form entries—1.2% likely human—and falling. The rest, 98.8%, a rising horde picking at the lock, stacking up in the yard. How did this happen? The site's been under attack a week. Somewhere out there, bots tapping keys behind doors, harder each day—the graph spikes into new realms, slowing down the server.

What can I do? Each night—more attempts. Each day—some slip through. When they make it, the network snuffs them. Too many. Too soon. They spew garbage for 9 seconds before—*killed*. A few impossible names make it into the logs—caught in the backups.

I block IPs. Like batting a hornet's nest. Some urgent fire ignites the bastions. The light bulb flickers—a pattern in the WiFi. All the hacked laptops humming together in the dark—the weight of dead voices pinging, just ghosts filling out forms in the night, to be remembered.

2.

Today was quieter. The curves tapering, less urgent. The storm of bots drifted to some new industry. Only a few, out of place and desperately seeking, showed up to query if we remember some forgotten glory between old friends—ones who would never tell— how they, though finally indicted for insurance fraud, had broken their friendship, and a family, to pieces. Having hit upon someone whose name was close enough to a memory, a shattered dream, 4 a.m., at the end of long searching, confessed into this contact form.

The careful fingers of such men make it past the SPAM filters every time. They persist, beneath our concern. Have we anything to fear more than ourselves? Lost in this tangled mess, unstuck in time, each polite form a fragile echo reaching further into the void.

Why not? Ask something of the void, though it be logged and archived in the steely certainty of indistinct data centers.

Reckonings

Certain Lightnings

     Row 34—
black window
     jet engine
       carving the air beside me
homeward
                       somewhere over Kentucky
Medallions of white light
linked by peach gridlines
drift behind the wing

                    a storm cloud appears—
     belching sow   scattering sparks
         a hundred miles off
     Flashes—
ghost the fuselage
rattle cloud-lips
         shadowing the engine's curve

The unfathomable—
         next flash
    the planet tries
      to arc its heart
        back to the sun

I ravel the world
        back
to certain lightnings
        that've struck
    in my mind—

Once plasma bloomed
          across permafrost
    antlers linked
        in a chain of light
three hundred reindeer
lit by one white spark

                collapsed in truce
      on tundra

Contemplating split atoms—
        the world itself
    all tantrums

            Indianapolis downpour
Two friends drunk
      howl curses
      into the bridge belly
            echo

Fuck you, God   for silence—
your faith   on the wire
not mine
       Bridge sizzle—
wrought iron
           singing ozone
     no message
        only static
thunder rebound
        up the canal and back
    clapped our heads
        cans crumbled
    beneath the span

darker now
     where light once frayed
Everything—nothing—
       rippling together

Soft
     A blast across the dune face—
Glass lightning bones
       crumb
          from the bluff

Slow rumble
            torn down by ricochet—
sotto voce afterthoughts—
                        a blacksmith
        dismantling the sky

You see behind me
                        I behind you
Flash—bang—
            everywhere at once

The house   shakes hidden bones
                Three blocks over—
a branch explodes
                The cats scatter
        thrown
            off the furniture
        out of that old world—
        welded
            in an implacable   truce—
                        tingling
            into tomorrow

Pawpaw Grove

The fruit of my homeland, deep in the forest,
down on the sandy creek bend.
A new tree rises the same—
spinning through seasons in shadow,
under slender cover of its source,

weathering storm surges,
learning the rhythm to hold fast
among stones in a creekside seep.

First purple flowers at the crown,
out of reach before any green,
three deep leaves around three lobes

bowing toward the blowfly—
a dark perfume pleads:
scatter my promise.

Crowns burst from every tip,
growing near the trickle,
sprinkling prisms of light
that shiver the pond.

Mud memory murmurs as waters recede,
recalling every face and season
pressed into garlands,
folded by circumstance,

bark finely writ by years
carries our laughter, our grief.
Here—

the golden pulp
of my homeland—
sweetness
and the bitter seed.

Intensive Care

I felt you in my heart,
ratchet moaning.
I heard you weeping
in the dark night of your mind—

remote ecstasy of suffering,
still functioning,
worried love piped into your skull,
monitored by color-coded squads:

teal who care,
burgundy who don't,
sky blue at the lungs,
royal blue at the heart.

Tubes lead back
to hanging bags,
rows silently drip.

Between emergencies,
ghosts complain
about ordinary dying.

Grape and wine uniforms
share a laugh on the floor.

In bed,
you are apart from us
tethered to beeping pumps
that live you towards life.

A symphony of clues—
no answers.
This body chained to this bed—

Alive to the promises
we keep

until you twitch
shock and shimmer,
details splitting apart—

eyes open—

You wake up.

Of Cowbirds and Sparrows

The cowbird lays its egg in another's nest,
and leaves it to fate.

The cowbird flies
but comes back quick.
Shooed again, but
used to it.

From birth, the sparrows cursed
but fed the stranger all the same—
rehearsed, endured—became
cruelties imagined in shame.

Color too dark,
knowing nothing but nest.
Tongue tuned deeper—
cut off from the rest.

Song in a different key
no one cares to hear.
Cries out just the same,
hardened by their jeers.

The cowbird too sure a sparrow
deeper, harder, knowing—
each time they say no
a truer sparrow growing.

Inside the wing, feathers—
deeper still, a bone lance.
What can the sparrow know
of its own excellence?

In the one song
made of all songs
we sing on
to right our wrongs.

Why not them most of all?
Concerns unheard,
born to endless complaints—
The scorned cowbird.

And when in time
the skies relent—
another cowbird's
appeals un-pent—

First light they share
will be their song—
In that soft hour
they'll belong.

History

What I say is true
You die, I die

This is for those who come after
So they will know
what happened here

— *Yellow Wolf, Nez Perce*

Steel-clawed men dig
the street in front of our house—
pull old garbage from deep down.

Jumble of slighted pipes stacked,
bulbous orange-crusted cudgels
once slept raw in dream-deep dirt.

Replacements sit, blued, waiting,
consigned in turn to darkness
for the future to puzzle over.

Workmen set bits of interest on the corner—
artifacts from inside the ditch,
a previous century's dump beneath us.

Old bottles, blue copper dirt—
scraps barely clinging to form—
lives long gone, mineralizing beneath the maple.

Here is my stub of a post and the hole I dug deep,
last scrap of concrete where the gate once stood,
a puddle, a seep, a crack begun—my doing.

This old garbage ravine
once hosted an ancient hunt—scarred this parcel
enough to leave some stone-bone remnants deep.

Most of what preceded us
failed to arrive whole—a flow still—
thin trickle trained down the drain.

What fights the grind—the grist
that wears the wheel—some universal thread
unbroken still, gristle no blade can shear.

None could wrest this thing from its idea—
Such mysteries persist,
undefeatable.

Ground beneath all our steps,
solemnity haunts the drainage—
We must live with it.

Extinct

My casual awe
wouldn't have saved you, ivory-billed
woodpecker—
gone now for good.

Cousin to pileated,
you once danced down old pitch pines
to hammer rattle rhythm
head first hard into heartwood,

to pluck delicate secrets
from the tree's heart
with spatula and tong
for profit.

Grander still—your ivory plumes,
Liberace woodpecker.
What would you sing for our time,
had we not made hats of you?

Goodbye raucous forest plunderer—
hushed from the heavens.
I imagine your glorious wings
casting a misty gloss

above towering trees,
each of you—plucked and prized
for the jealous goddess—Vanity.
Beauty was your doom.

Giant sequoias not tall enough
to crown the flames of human commerce
leave us witness,
worshipping ash outlines in drifting sand.

All songs stretch to dirges as the music drains.
Time forgets us—each, in turn,
what can we do but abide the loss
though beauty's martyr should be avenged somehow.

Kingfisher still finds dragonfly.
Heron at dusk, lone fish lord,
still twists his sinuous neck—
jabs—pierce—

Surely your spirit still flickers
here, somewhere.
Might you still inspire
a fragile glory?

Cockleshells and Terrorsaur Bones

Deep water
carves out the stiff stone.

Pressure bounces back—
spring-loaded recoil

river's long labor
peeling limestone—

Cockleshells
and terrorsaur bones,
giant ferns dug out—

memories harden into certainty,
bone-grit reborn in stone

fused, crushed—
the long labor
of tectonics

mash,
bulge,
pinch,

continent's steady crush
meets future's meltwater flow

spilling down
from snow-lined stone—

thin tumble down
glacier-fed,
lake-saturated earth—

Time's thrust—
a burrowing worm
of oblivion,
sure pressure against the past.

A breath,
a wind—
drink it in,
collapse—

Splash
swirling *sanctus*.

Brief Kings

Rulers,
born of rules,
sing their dominion.

Brief kings,
crowned by promises
opposed to nature—

their songs quiver
in the rain trough's hollow.
Down in the chill of miasma,

flushed out from seed—
water-split seams
erupt from earth grip

Brute blush of life
lifts the stalk
by ratchet and pulse

purple pressures
reach out for the sun's warmth,
clinging along crags to catch rays.

Even you, burst from filth,
press green charge
toward crimson spray.

The Mountain

We sit together, listening—
      inside a calving cloud
            along a talus-mantled ridge.

Pillow mist condenses
      over lichen-covered
            sheets of toppled chances.

With each thaw, new slabs
      shear off the ridge—
            bent to the wind

hurtled merciless
      scratched ticket
            falling.

Everything slides,
      the sagging mass of millennia
            presses down off the top.

No mountain left—
      just us, watching.
            Nowhere left to climb.

Sky opens—
      a green carpet
            to the far ridge.

San Juans before us—
      Hesperus rising
            across a sweep of scree.

Another mountain—
      Here to there in sight
            the journey long still.

Parsimonious rock-hop
        picking our way down,
                dog bounding first.

A family of goats below
        watching to see
                what will become of us.

Marmot chirps
        bounce across the valley.
                Sheep ready to move.

We slip back into the trees,
        the air humid with life again—
                tepid column—breath of cedar.

The dog rushes through,
        savoring every breath that speaks,
                his joy beyond all scolding.

Flash—
        Stone-mountain lightning.
                A bell ringing far off,

the din still arriving,
        almost nothing—
                grumble of what could be.

Collapsing the I

Walk the sand, crusted by frost.
Scuff shadowy smudges
through brittle light filigree

undercut by collapses,
left strung in ice-thread lattice—
that brief self

before a brush of wind
bursts all bravado
back to basics.

I am
collapsing
into I.

The universe stalls—
Whatever violence urges the spin
resolves to stillness—

Stops.
All certainties of space bind—
stand—a single jewel moment

every seed slung—
every bloom blown—
every last fruit hung—

unwound to nothing—
The last atom lets go
its desperate charm.

Quarks drift off,
forgetting their grip
as we do—
cast to ruins,

gone now,
gone—
Gone.

Billionaires

Huge beasts block the downfall
far away.
You must drive the world
to find them—

react in darkness
to a sound
from the trees—

the world
inevitable,
something that would always flower
if the clay were roughened.

A quiver
in the lightest breath
would bloom
with fresh chances.

Separations
behind kind regards
twist our delicate
eager hearts—

while titans glower
stiff as statues
in far too far corners—

trapped in
mountain memberships,
all courtesies withheld.

Scaffolding theories into the void—
Giants mutter their slow thoughts.
Shapes dissolve into dusk.
Clouded conspiratorial monsters

holding silent accord in the great beyond,
taught to yearn for stasis in dread of emptiness.

They stir the pot—
so slowly
you can't be sure.

They say they do
and the dust never settles.

Humanitas

1

Beneath a name, there is a body—
a grim human display,
meant to stir more disgust
than fear.

An indifferent hand
does this work.

Two figures not yet risen—
she in nightgown,
he still buttoning his pants,
staring past the porch light,

No sigh escapes
to rouse the wind.

The night crosses over.
Gallows madmen,
brains baked in their boxes,
howl while they still can.

2

The white coats
deep in study
survey the body, mapped
and flung open on the table—

make note—
All one.

Belted ankles.
Hands strapped across.
Noose lifted.

all one
all one

Every window repeats
the scene.

shanti shanti shanti.

3
Beneath the atom, a grid.
Beneath the grid,
the detritus of language.

All matters offered
as words—
tangled,
unfinished.

4
Cut to the bone,
blood at the lip
not yet spilt.

I steady my hand.

Drones are bombing children.
I drink my coffee.

My heart
twists, then relents.

Somewhere in a dark garage,
a compressor
kicks on.

Freedom

1. Sun
in a hammock slung
out of the sun,
outside history—
What is freedom?

Bird in the sky.
Cat in the garden.
A grace of slow, unfolding time.

Sitting with blood-red gladiolas,
raised from clean seed,
kitchen-window witness
straining to eat the sun.

I saw freedom
charge toward sacrifice.
This privilege
of new wreckage—

free to light one off,
watch it sputter into the sky,
die a glorious red bloom
recalling old victories,

new reasons to accept.
Free to move on.
Sun-beaten glory.

2. Debt
Freedom cast in brass, eagle-shaped,
traded for safety, comfort, nutrition.

Join debts and sorrow/joy
To tour from a camper on a hitch.

Free to roam on credit leash.
Free to wear the collar.

$50 in pocket over IPAs,
idea-swapping tongues glisten—
a new moon rising, blind possibility.

Dollars sound out your days.
First you must purchase
a favorable horoscope.
Freedom.

3. Fire
His craven sneer,
bucking regiment,
licking ice cream
unleashed on freedom's
off-road rampage.

Freedom stripped
with a rough tongue,
put to task,
recast in shade.

Returned on the inside,
in love, free together.
A prayer seed to worry
in penance.

Naked as a jaybird—
just like the day
you were born.

Free hard fury of grace,
chalice in hand,
savage laugh in the throat—

Beach fire—
flames torment the chill night
inside this entire galaxy!

4. Voice
Liberty's breath,
the radio,
a compressed cry—

Free to meet the sun,
stand before the rest,
intone for all of us
your hard progress.

These strong songs
bark you awake
every morning—

carried out to carry on,
broke like always, rattled
on your stark train.

Free of memory
before death's done.
Free to forget
before the sun.

A rigorous silence,
cut by horizons,
shames every soft refrain
to crickets.

5. *After*
Cry labor's hard song—
lemon, fire,
ash, and smoke.

A song for free people
once writ on tatters,
now run beyond rags.

Blown down by sorrow
wishing joy for all
but pounding out folly
bound to sing.

Free to begin again.
A final egress arranged.
Nothing resolved.
Mistakes erased.

Soul impressed
with new wisdom
beyond our own discoveries,

tuned by desire
until suffused with ecstasy,
dreams gathered at the ankle—
made honey, made bee.

Grand Rapids

The south land tumbles—
ground-up earth, shed
from the crust of cliff glaciers.

The carved face of a two-mile ice wall
sheds eternal water, wide as our science.

The grand cosmic rapids
hide at dawn.

Sun breaks open the clouds—
a radiant flood

topples ice towers,
sheds diamond cathedrals.

Blue ice blades spat from deep
drown and rise again,

stab out from the crust
to fling boulders over fen.

Now they are here—
Caw, caw, caw—elusive spirits

twirl vapor beneath wings
unconcerned with catastrophe.

A glimmer appears in the wave pool
where the torrent's mind collapses.

Just before it gives way to words
a glint off the wing of the sky.

A spirit in the water,
not yet named, listens.

Nestled in the current—a new color—
an eye not yet conceived to see it.

When You Tried to Die

for the suicides

Adjoining orchards set my own ablaze—
Not dirt, but bruise-darkened hands
recall the sweetest fruits.

Was I once
or was that you—
afraid to taste the apricots?
I'll burn my words and start anew.

You came to me however you could,
so I held you as if I could hold you still—
a shiver quaking inside my chest.

We chose this fruit to ripen,
to learn such greatness together—
Now the sweetness burns off in the wind.

Abolish time, repeat our courtesies.
When another cruel-eyed moon rises
you would end it all.

Shall we taste the stone instead?
Left from a persistent worry—hard pit
that will not burn or sorrow us.

I'm left to love
the schist more ancient than life—
nothing to keep,
nothing to throw away.

So linger on—
Tell me more—
Even our curses must be of some use.

Openings

Wind Rose

for Christine

Had we sung before this?
Had we danced?
I was straddling a rooftop
finding a new way to you,

drinking the cooking sherry,
singing to the trees,
in love with you—
my wind rose.

Cured of confusion
about death's ruin,
the dark's disdain—
just a boy on a bender.

Did I ask you to save me?
Just see me—
You chose the rest.
I was fool enough to chance it

chasing the cat along the roof crest,
the sunset wailing
through the trees.
You were the wind rose.

You let me back in
through the window,
cat in hand—
All of us intact.

Totality

Daylight falters—sky drops.
Will this darkness end?
Whispers ripple star-struck, stunned.

No secret now—
A firestorm's signet
stamps the sky.

Ravaged by doubt,
on the brink of reckoning,
we watch old scars ease open—

New darkness—
stranger than death,
deeper than the deepest sleep.

Tender new doubts bloom,
despite our bright vain beliefs,
as we give over to totality—

terror, awe, a brief reunion—
whispering together
beneath a hollow sun.

A dark searchlight
cuts through shadows—
the long grave-chill.

Listen—birdsong, whispers—
old friends scraping songs
from dreams and shed sorrow,

shot through the heart
by cosmic rays,
our silences burning through.

Black wings rise from the ether, calling.
Each living thing
offers no answer.

Deep sight stiffens the gaze.
The ring reveals more possibilities.
What darkness hollows the heart of us?

Spark: new dawn.
Moon bows out.
Daylight again.
As ever before.

We who screech like owls,
too wise for mercy,
too lost for spite,

we watched the sun go out
and imagined her loss
pierced us deeper still.

Energy Fossil

1
Looking down over Georgia—
fire-spotting shadows,
riding blasted air towards night.

Great spinning Kali
goddess of time and flame
burns this galaxy
in the cathedral void to my left.

A Mondrian patchwork
where the cattails drown,
contrails over Walmart halo
in the red wash of a local sunset.

2
Starlight
carried through vast darkness.
Inside the energy—
an eternal core.

All apparent colors,
spectrum spread,
move with me
in my eye.

Each moment,
everywhere—
from here to there.

My light
winds in your light.

Red coals beam—
corona effluvia,
carbon song.

Starry torch
evicts an arc
of orange.

Brazen rads
etch a blue sky.

Shadow, be sure—
Toss down
what is not you.

This promise
runs deep.

Yellow acid
eats most evidence.

How will you live?
Go on in echo.

A starlit melody
at midnight
will suffice.

Lay down within the scene
beneath the actors.

The air unmoved
is the wind
regardless.

Hazy Cloud

I hit the brakes—
white tail flagging
inches out of reach—

the edge of ending,
a stutter in time.

Lucky.

Forewarned,
the deer leaps off—

Darkness moves
among the signposts.

Fog-banked curves—
Ottawa Chief Hazy Cloud's
Old hunting grounds
along the Thornapple.

4 a.m.,
heading west into town.

I reach for

words
unbidden,

words
for you alone:

> *E la le. e la le.*
> *E la le. e la le.*

Mathematics of Longing

Organizing principles
for this resolution
of irrationals—

Molecules arranging
a mute streak
of certainties.

One principle pulls together
the severed membrane,
drawing me to your smile.

Gather the river from me.
Don't look back for promises,
ageless stranger.

All loyalties are just a crush—
against crush—
filling empty pockets.

Patterns arise.
Adorn yourself
with the provenance of oceans.

Surrender whole—
Part only
upon strong stone.

Leave no voice
in the sand.

Sing seismic
intimations of dusk
until we prove tomorrow.

Lake Superior Woman

for Christine

Lake Superior woman
loves you
like a birch
in spring catkins.

The boulders
laugh and play
all century
beneath her waves.

She offers me stones
now smooth, fondled for ages
by storm-warmed hands,
I roll them on my tongue,

standing on the point
further out near the sky,
where spiders and driftwood
gather watchful of all time,

drawn by the rise
of an inescapable shadow,
the sun—a distant burn
quenching in her body,

in the last dim slip,
I search her agate eyes—
and promise myself
to her dawn.

When she lets me
inside her
a new blaze builds
till I am completely hers—

Foamy flesh,
the beach quivers—
as if a great eagle
had flown over.

When she turns to me
my bones are glowing.
My old wound—a great sigh
released into her mists—

carried over her horizon,
until I disappear into her breath.

Shine

Sieves clatter clogged
with bits of shine—

fragments of dreams
that won't wash away—

heavy gold
fleck in the pan.

The day dawns dingy.
Myriad motes
hang onto each other—

While the rust
of generations compounds—

squealing, moaning,
chemically excited—
ground to base shapes.

Day grimy with words,
endless thoughts,
sand rolling down an incline
towards stable ground.

One day,
all things fall enough
to one side or the other—

facts parse into truth,
encode in beauty,
shine in the pan.

Surf Being Born Free Enough

Gather signatures on checks
while ye may.
Make payments with purpose.

Heal the saddle sores of commerce.
Apocalypse warren
free of foxes.

Decoy salesmen cross deserts,
climb mountains
to pitch you.

Surf being born free enough,
new dawn market
writes the headlines:

A vetted assembly adrift by noon—
A rag washed along by a current—
endings rearranged.

Emerging life from life—
energy intact, birthplace burning,
free to rage or quench—

Foolscap ledger burned—
ash enough for the roses.
Surf, being born free enough.

Ode to π

Irrational truth
of time's circumference,
you let us walk full three

and just that one
fragmented defense—
agreed.

But why expend
your infinite originality
in endless flight?

Step over and accept
what the approximate reveals.

In your grace
looped about yourself—
tangled Greek signs
carved to hold secrets—

a vague rule shapes itself
to nature,
stumbles
that last little bit—

The foolish fragment
always spits out another.

The bottomless pit
invents itself again,

spits a number—
more true, more useless—

carries on ensuring circles
long after curiosity relents.

My Zombie Novel

In my zombie novel, there is a princess who gets no rest along the palace balustrades where her father once grew monkeys and tigers but now only tea and dread.

One day the sky went strange—green butterflies flew over, coughing coins into everyone's upturned faces. Her father was blinded, and dashed to the ground, and rose again—changed, as if his dreams had come true.

In my zombie novel, the undead are really men broken by despair, dreaming only of the princess, arriving at all hours to marvel at her shadow. Everyone's part-dead, partly alive. It's told from the perspective of a princess whom everyone adores. Zombies, like lumbering power tools, rattle across the floor, in search of love or brains.

It's true—I'm like her father, sifting sand from hand to hand like a tired hourglass, hunting some forgotten fragment that could still save us. And it's true—you're like the princess who may not exist, or hides so well no one can prove her real.

In my zombie novel, the king throws open the palace doors to a shambling horde—legendary in the decayed minds of the undead, tangling in the great hall like a many-armed god of hope, offering protest, and death, and peace.

The horde falls in love with the idea of the princess they never once glimpsed. She only wants to be left alone. She'd rather be sand—drift on the wind and pepper their eyes with sleep—my eyes most of all.

No one wants to read this zombie novel. They're too busy dreaming of princesses of their own whittled by winds down to their most exquisite parts.

Somehow a man stumbles through a doorway. All the human burden returns on him, knob in hand. His heart a padlock scarred by crowbars. His greeting is hoarse and sticks in his throat. The door locked for good. Everyone's always reaching towards a fire, or any other remnant of the ancient world that isn't strong enough to save them—but saves another moment. Far from the heaven of a kind word, he recalls the crisp turn of a smile—yet still locked.

The princess comes alive like a fire. He calls to her, promising tiaras. He pleads for her to reign over his heart. Sincere by nature, he asks for the right things even at the wrong times—with the wrong people.

They look at each other—man and woman—despite everything: her undead father lying slain between them, the green butterflies dropping golden coins, being written from the sand against their will.

They ask me: "Why? Why is this happening? Why do you do this to us?"

I, their father—who wrote them out of the void, say: "Leave me alone. I want to live. I've given you too much already."

In my zombie novel, green butterflies flocked the sky. Their coins fell like blows, raining on my head—a new promise beyond defeat.

What answers are good enough? They give their lives to us. "I have let green butterflies into my room. I was gathering their golden coins for your dowry. Now—dance."

Before Me, You

for Christine

You before me—
New moon silent we
before I
took breath.
Heart-cast
five first years
before us.
This song—
laughter,
love-scorched,
unlocking our
future breath—
Our life—
a night song
begun from silence
to inspire
arriving
ingenious
dawn.
We
before
us—
sky before stars—
An echo leading beyond—
what we sing now
to the future.

From the Bath

The mind-machine marks
the anniversary of a bee sting,
counts every tingle, to be sure.

She sings downstairs—
strums her uke—
learning new chords.

Inside my body,
everything talks to itself,
limps out of sequence, getting the news.

The mind replays inelegant choices,
re-knits patterns on the fly,

simulates humiliations to toughen the heart,
stitches and stitches—
old wounds into scars.

Inside, the rules stay strict—
take hold of timid organelles
break out molecular regiments

drive membranes to burst
in metabolic mills

to warm the bones or sing a song.
All this rush and tyranny—
to wash a dish, make coffee.

A fortress-heart under siege.
A body flush with magnesium,
taken by song.

Her voice climbs the stairs.
"Dust in the wind / All we are"

The mind must relent—

A spark of unceasing
green light draws ahead

asking before asking,
telling before telling.

The thinnest tuft of down
in the crib's pillow,
the mind-machine recalls—

We are woven in silk to our tips.
"Just a drop of water in an endless sea"

My chest rises / falls
with the glow of mineral truth.

Inside everything its opposite
reflects a contrary note—

Fear and hope pressed thin
between layers of onionskin.

Discernment
born of necessity
matches intent to intensity.

"All our dreams
crumble to the ground
though we refuse to see"

She calls plaintively,
not to me—
to the universe—

I swallow the last
crumbs of mind.

Such a gift—to rise
ego-sated, from the bath—

The floor secure,
the stairs intact,
The air still kind.

Author Bio

Scott Krieger is a poet, novelist, and designer based in Grand Rapids, Michigan, where he lives with his wife, the poet Christine Stephens-Krieger, and their three cats. Krieger is the author of the novel *Illyrian Fugue* and has completed several other manuscripts of poetry and fiction. He is active in the local arts community, serving as co-president of the Grand River Poetry Collective and its publishing imprint, Grand River Poetry Press.

Acknowledgements

Aside from live performances of early drafts of *Freedom* and *Grand Rapids* at open mic events, all these poems make their first appearance here.

I'm grateful to my peer group of poets in the Grand River Poetry Collective who showed me what a book of poetry could be both through their direct feedback and the example of their own work. Christine Stephens-Krieger, Barbara Saunier, David Cope, Melissa Wray, Neil Kaufman, Leslie Papp, Katie Kalisz, Estelle Slootmaker, Nellie deVries, Camille Newsom, Lamont Arrington, Sarah Clarissa Mieras, Thomas Gregory Bliss, Mursalata Muhammad, Donna Munro, Shayna Marie. Thank you for your generous spirit and solidarity in solitary work.

I'm grateful for the enduring friendships that have guided me, Nathan Filbert, Thomas Henry, John Winkelman, Von Franklin, Hugo Claudin, John Smieska, Curt Witteveen, Liem Nguyen, Salem Joseph, Tim Calkins, Andy Weber, who continue to shape my life as we ring together like chimes in a long deep song.

To those who have passed through on their way to something further, Jeff Boughner, Al Thayer, Stephen Durst, Yen Hoa Lee, Ralph S. Louis, mentors still. I salute you.

To my wife, Christine, my partner in all things. She has offered guidance to my soul, my mind and my words. We grow from this place together out into the world. I am born of the love we share. Thank you, my love.

Notes

A few concepts warrant some explanation:

Sipapu is a small hole in the floor of a kiva symbolic for the hole from the underworld through which Ancestral Puebloans climbed out to reach this world. There are many examples in the American Southwest at sites like Mesa Verde and Chaco Canyon.

Kairos is a reference to the early Ancient Greece god of the opportune moment. He is not quite fortune, not quite fate. Perhaps something closer to panache. He has wings and hair in a reverse mullet. As he winks by, on the most beneficial path, you must grab him by his forelock, for he has no hair behind and if you cannot get before him, you're chance is lost. Hold onto his forelock and you can ride the Kairos wind.

WLS is a legendary AM radio station out of Chicago that on certain clear nights in the 1970s, could reach across Lake Michigan, bounce off the atmosphere and come to my old radio at 3 am, bringing jazz in lieu of sleep.

Bastinado is a corporal punishment involving the beating of the bottoms of the feet.

Djinn is a reference to gin and the genie.

Shanti is a Sanskrit word meaning peace. Repeated three times to invoke deep, enduring peace in the body, mind, and spirit.